Coloring Test Area

© Copyright 2020 Misery Loves Coloring™ & NorthGeeks, LLC

YOU ARE A
NATURAL
DISASTER

DEAD
INSIDE

YOU WILL DIE ALONE

IN DOG YEARS YOU'RE DEAD

NO...
NO NO YOU
CAN'T.

EVERYTHING'S FUCKED

MY POOR LIFE CHOICES CAN BE USED AS A BAD EXAMPLE

CRIPPLING DEPRESSION IS MY SUPERPOWER!

Life Is Shit
With Sprinkles
On Top

#YOUSUCK

KEEP THAT
SHIT
BOTTLED UP

TEXT BOOK DEFINITION OF:
SOCIALLY AKWARD
BUT
MORALLY FLEXIBLE

LIFT ME UP HIGHER
SO I CAN FALL FARTHER

FACE
OF AN
ANGEL
BODY
OF
REGRET

HIDE
THE PAIN
&
SEEK
SOME MORE

JUST GOT OUT OF THE SHOWER, LOOKS LIKE LIFE STILL STINKS

RADIATE
NEGATIVE

cloudy with a chance of dystopia
SAVE THE FUCKING KOALAS

GO AWAY
I WENT OUTSIDE ONCE AND DIED INSIDE

OL • BALL • POOL • BAI
JUST WADING IN
A CESSPOOL OF
POOR CHOICES

VETERINARIAN
FREE NEUTERING
AN EXISTENTIAL CRISIS IS CLOSER THAN IT APPEARS

JUST MORE BULLSHIT HANGING OVER MY HEAD

HELLO
my name is
EMOTIONALLY
DEGRADABLE

I'M A SAD SHITTY RAINBOW

You are beyond help.

like gravity
i will drag
you down

A SHOOTING STAR!
I WISH I WAS DEAD.

IT'S COOL TO NOT HAVE FRIENDS TO SHARE MY SADNESS AND ICE CREAM WITH.

THANKS FOR PLAYING.

www.ingramcontent.com/pod-product-compliance
Lightning Source LLC
Chambersburg PA
CBHW080004180726
48002CB00020B/2999